EINKORN COOKBOOK

Simple and Delicious Einkorn Recipes for Every Home Baker

Todd S. Ashurst

Table of Contents

CHAPTER 1

EINKORN FLOUR RECIPES RANKED ALL-TIME BEST

Einkorn flour is a non-hybridized old wheat assortment. I've accumulated the best einkorn flour recipes so you can without much of a stretch take a shot at utilizing this better grain. Certain individuals use einkorn 1:1 for current wheat flour, however I find that doesn't necessarily work. That is the reason I got some margin to allot einkorn and tried these recipes to guarantee the best outcomes. I'll likewise share how to trade ordinary flour for einkorn flour in your #1 recipes, on the grounds that once you begin baking with einkorn, it will immediately turn into your #1 flour

Any recipe you would ordinarily utilize wheat flour in you can utilize einkorn! It has a high protein content, however it has less versatility than present day wheat. I suggest beginning with cakes, flapjacks (I'll share an extraordinary recipe to begin with toward the finish of this article), and biscuits, since yeast can be somewhat precarious to work with in einkorn. When you're OK with making biscuits, cake, and flapjacks, continue on to einkorn sandwich bread made with fast yeast or sourdough einkorn bread.

At the point when you buy einkorn flour, search for "generally useful" on the mark. Joyful Foods Einkorn All-Purpose Flour is my #1 flour and the most straightforward to track down in the United States. You can get one single pack or a 10-lb mass sack. This implies a portion of the wheat has been eliminated and it will act all the more near the regular baking flour you are utilized to. You'll see the flour is somewhat more yellow, so your prepared products may be a marginally unexpected variety in comparison to normal too. Assuming that you like to utilize entire wheat einkorn, you can find out about baking with this flour in the FAQ segment or in the tip box beneath.

If you're spic and span to einkorn and have any desire to look further into the historical backdrop of this antiquated grain and the issue with present day wheat, look at What is Einkorn? Furthermore, Tips for Using Einkorn Flour and pay attention to my digital broadcast about einkorn and gluten delicate.

Could I at any point eat einkorn wheat assuming I have celiac sickness?

No! This is certainly some deception I have seen around. Einkorn IS wheat and it contains gluten (albeit a frail gluten structure, it actually contains wheat and gluten). The old grain is by and large more straightforward for individuals to process on the off chance that they have a minor narrow mindedness. I personally find I can endure sourdough (which includes maturing grains prior to consuming) or einkorn a lot simpler than different types of wheat. In any case, on the off chance that you have a hazardous sensitivity or celiacs, you won't have any desire to eat einkorn. Carla, the organizer behind Jovial Foods, began reaping and delivering einkorn flour due to her little girl's gluten awarenesses (stand by listening to her story in this digital broadcast episode).

CHAPTER 2

ADVANTAGES OF EINKORN FLOUR

I've done the examination and expounded a great deal on the advantages of einkorn! Here are a portion of the top advantages of loading and utilizing einkorn flour in your genuine food kitchen...

• More straightforward to Digest: Ancient grains, as einkorn, are simpler to process than present day wheat assortments. Individuals with gluten sensitives (not celiacs, einkorn isn't without gluten) find that einkorn is simpler to process because of its extremely powerless gluten structure.

• Simple to Substitute: Once you've made a couple of recipes, it's extremely simple to substitute generally useful einkorn for your typical regular flour.

• Great Nutritional Profile: Einkorn has a high protein content (30% higher than current wheat), less starch (15% not exactly present day wheat), and contains carotenoids, minerals, and B nutrients.

• No Knead: Einkorn could do without to be complained

with or massaged like wheat flour. For breads and rolls (for example cinnamon rolls, sandwich bread, and cheeseburger buns) that generally require a long massaging process, your arms can enjoy some time off and let einkorn do something amazing.

Could I at any point substitute einkorn flour for customary flour?

If you have a most loved recipe and need to take a stab at utilizing einkorn rather than entire wheat or generally useful normal flour, this is the way to do that. Einkorn might be involved cup for cup in recipes calling for entire wheat flour while making biscuits, flapjacks, treats, and cakes. While making these recipes, you might have to lessen the fluid sum (like the milk) by 15%. Einkorn assimilates fluid gradually. Permit einkorn player to rest for 10 minutes prior to adding to a biscuit, bread, or cake dish. Assuming that following 10 minutes of rest, you feel more flour is required, add more einkorn right now.

CHAPTER 3

FREE EINKORN BAKING GUIDE

Figure out how to prepare like an expert and make the best bread, treats, biscuits, flapjacks, and that's just the beginning!

SEND IT MY WAY!

10 Best Einkorn Flour Recipes

Most loved Einkorn Recipes

- Einkorn Pizza Dough

- Einkorn Master Muffin Recipes

- Einkorn Pancakes

- Einkorn Chocolate Chip Cookies

- Einkorn Chocolate Cake

- Einkorn Tortillas

- Einkorn Banana Muffins

- Einkorn Sandwich Bread

- Einkorn Sugar Cookies

- Einkorn Chicken and Dumpling Soup

The flavor and surface of einkorn flour means the most tasty, simpler to-process heated merchandise, from cake and cupcakes to treats to soup dumplings and scones and biscuits. The majority of the recipes on this rundown are made with universally handy einkorn flour, yet entire wheat einkorn may likewise be utilized (lessen the entire wheat einkorn by 1/4 cup). In the event that you're crushing einkorn berries to make flour at home, utilize the weight estimations (grams) versus cups gave in the recipes (this is undeniably more precise as newly processed flour will be light and vaporous).

1. Einkorn Pizza

You can undoubtedly make up an einkorn flour pizza batter that works perfectly on the barbecue or in the broiler. Simply add your #1 garnishes and supper is prepared instantly!

My children likewise love transforming the pizza batter into little flatbreads so they can have pizza lunchables for school. An even speedier choice is to make these Einkorn Pizza Muffins - you could without much of a stretch mistake the player and prepare these right subsequent to cooking your Homemade Einkorn Pizza Dough. That way you just cut up garnishes once and eat all set all week long.

Einkorn Pizza Dough

A simple to-make natively constructed pizza mixture made with generally useful einkorn flour.

MAKE THIS RECIPE

2. Einkorn Muffins

Biscuits are a number one in my home. I like that they are not difficult to alter in view of the fixings you want to go through; there's compelling reason need to go out and purchase anything exceptional. I made a Master Einkorn Muffin Recipe, particularly for this reason! You can decide to mix your extraordinary mixins into the hitter or tweak every biscuit whenever you've placed the player into the tin.

The expert einkorn biscuit recipe is one of the most-famous einkorn recipes. This is what JR, from the Live Simply Community, needed to say, "My significant other and I are beginning our 'genuine food' venture. You and your site have been really useful, and this biscuit recipe was our most memorable baking experience. My better half has consistently had a gift for baking, so I've been unimaginably honored over the course of the years with all that she does. We both concurred these biscuits were, by a long shot, the best thing she's consistently heated. The flavors are all so rich and genuine. Much obliged such a great amount for all your time put into helping other people begin practicing good eating habits, genuine food! You're a colossal gift!"

In the event that you're not feeling inventive on making your own assortments, I have parts to browse:

- Lemon Poppy Einkorn Muffins

- Einkorn Cinnamon Roll Muffins

- Einkorn Banana Muffins

- Einkorn Pumpkin Spice Muffins

- Einkorn Chocolate Zucchini Muffins

Einkorn Master Muffin Recipe: One Recipe, Multiple Possibilities

An expert einkorn biscuit recipe with different blend in

potential outcomes. Make these biscuits your own by adding your number one blend ins, similar to: chocolate chips, natural product, nuts, or destroyed coconut.

MAKE THIS RECIPE

3. Einkorn Dumpling Soup

Chicken and dumpling soup is a chilly climate solace food staple, even here in Florida. There's only something about it that makes me grin when we eat it. One of my number one pieces of making Einkorn Chicken and Dumpling Soup is the way that the "dumplings" cook squarely in the stock. There's compelling reason need to turn on the broiler and messy additional baking dishes, just drop your hitter into the percolating soup, cover, and pause!

CHAPTER 4

BEST HOMEMADE EINKORN CHICKEN AND DUMPLING SOUP

Einkorn Chicken and Dumpling Soup is our #1 soup to appreciate in the colder time of year. The BEST hand crafted chicken soup I've made, and when the soup is finished off with rich einkorn dumplings... flawlessness!

MAKE THIS RECIPE

4. Einkorn Cake

Einkorn functions admirably in cakes. The generally useful adaptation, when filtered, makes the best crumb.This Honey-Sweetened Applesauce Carrot Cake is the ideal occasion show. In the event that you like chocolate, certainly attempt Einkorn Chocolate Cake in a sheet skillet. On the off chance that you need cake that is not difficult to serve for a party, make cupcakes! You can either do a one-bowl twofold chocolate assortment or pick exemplary vanilla cupcakes with buttercream icing.

This is the very thing that Brittni needed to say regarding making the einkorn chocolate cake, "I don't normally leave remarks on websites since I'm generally shy of time (mother life). Nonetheless, I needed to slip away briefly to remark since this is genuinely the best chocolate cake I've at any point had. I'm really particular and generally cake is great since it's chocolate cake, yet this cake is totally staggering. My young men are delicate to wheat yet can eat Einkorn. It has been an expectation to learn and adapt baking with it so I'm typically not expecting mind blowing with Einkorn recipes. In any case, we chose to check this recipe out after a speedy google look for my child's birthday. We were all exceptionally intrigued. The icing is past delectable. Genuinely the best icing I've at any point tasted. The cake is amazing in surface and flavor. With everything taken into account this recipe is a manager. Much obliged to you for sharing this recipe. We will utilize it numerous a lot more times."

Best Einkorn Chocolate Cake

A natively constructed chocolate cake made with einkorn flour. Rich, chocolatey, and impeccably improved, finished off with a hand crafted chocolate buttercream icing.

MAKE THIS RECIPE

5. Einkorn Pancakes and Waffles

Whether it's a languid end of the week early lunch or breakfast for supper, hotcakes are consistently a hit. Natively constructed Einkorn Pancakes rush to make and you can undoubtedly twofold them and freeze, making them a speedy breakfast choice or even packable for lunch.

Einkorn Pancakes

A make-ahead well disposed flapjack recipe made with old einkorn flour.

MAKE THIS RECIPE

Considerably simpler than flipping individual hotcakes is making it in a sheet dish! Assuming you've never done this, I strongly suggest it. These look wonderful on a plate finished off with new natural product slices.I have hardly any insight into you, yet my children have consistently cherished plunging things. Make breakfast involved by baking up a group of Easy Mini Pancake Muffins.

Heated Einkorn Sheet Pan Pancakes

Broiler prepared on a sheet skillet and made with einkorn flour. The ideal flapjack recipe for a bustling work day morning or when you need something speedy and simple toward the end of the week. Tweak as you would prefer with different garnishes or blend ins.

MAKE THIS RECIPE

Waffles made with einkorn are light and breezy with a great flavor and lovely brilliant tone (a quality of einkorn). This Einkorn Waffles recipe can be made utilizing generally useful or entire wheat einkorn.

Einkorn Waffles

This recipe is made with einkorn flour, an old grain, which

makes cushioned and light waffles that are ideal for a Sunday morning. Or on the other hand make the waffles ahead of time, hold up them, and appreciate consistently!

MAKE THIS RECIPE

6. Einkorn Tortillas

On the off chance that it's Taco Tuesday or you simply need a quick, simple bread for a sandwich, check Einkorn Tortillas out. Indeed, it is much more work than getting them at the store, however they look absolutely astonishing with the margarine and einkorn turning a beautiful yellow shade. I guarantee once you get ready they are easy to make and look exceptionally noteworthy. You can likewise transform them into tortilla pizzas for a supper where everybody makes their own pizza!

Einkorn Tortillas

Simple, basic fixing hand crafted tortillas made with einkorn flour. Make an enormous group toward the end of the week and save the extra to appreciate later in the week (store in the cooler) or freeze the additional items for a future feast.

MAKE THIS RECIPE

7. Einkorn Cookies

Everybody cherishes an exemplary chocolate chip treat or exemplary oats treat. I think treats are an extraordinary method for figuring out how to involve your scale for baking. Adding the fixings to your bowl without dirtying a lot of estimating cups and spoons is truly simple.

CHAPTER 5

EINKORN CHOCOLATE CHIP COOKIES

Natively constructed chocolate chip treats made with the old grain einkorn. Delicate, marginally chewy, and entirely thick. Exactly what a chocolate chip treat ought to be.

MAKE THIS RECIPE

In the event that you hate chocolate or oats treats, perhaps Soft and Chewy Einkorn Snickerdoodles are more your style. I likewise tried out einkorn in my number one Christmas treats on the grounds that the children love designing Einkorn Sugar Cookies. Or on the other hand, get the entire family engaged with making Einkorn Jam Thumbprint Cookies.

Exemplary Einkorn Oatmeal Cookies

The exemplary oats treat gets a tasty turn with this einkorn flour recipe. Made with less sugar, a lot of oats, warm flavors, and universally handy einkorn flour. Add your #1 blend in, similar to chocolate chips or raisins.

MAKE THIS RECIPE

8. Einkorn Sandwich Bread

I concede, I will frequently get bread from the market, particularly when it is sourdough. I love supporting these private ventures and bread simply appears to be so difficult to make, right? Be that as it may, I have had extraordinary achievement making Einkorn Bread with yeast. There's simply something so mysterious about watching the batter transcend the container, and nothing is superior to its fragrance heating up in the broiler. Make this for extraordinary events, particularly thickly cut and transformed into French toast!

Assuming you might want to make einkorn sourdough bread, I suggest this recipe from Jovial Foods.

Instructions to Make Einkorn Bread

There's nothing, in the kitchen, similar to the smell and satisfaction that comes from combining as one the fixings to make a yeast bread, watching the tacky mixture supernaturally twofold in size, and afterward take in the fragrance of the bread baking in the stove.

MAKE THIS RECIPE

Not sandwich bread, however worth focusing on here is cornbread. Einkorn makes the best cornbread to serve close by soups, a protein and veggie, or with no guarantees (since you need cornbread in your life)! Here is my skillet cornbread recipe utilizing generally useful einkorn flour.

Simple Homemade Skillet Einkorn Cornbread

Ideal for a warm bowl of soup or stew, this einkorn cornbread has a flavorful morsel. May likewise be made into biscuits.

MAKE THIS RECIPE

9. Einkorn Scones

Scones can truly lift your tea or espresso time. I think they are one of the most mind-blowing prepared merchandise for imparting to a gathering of companions in your home. They are extremely strong so they likewise travel well on the off chance that you are taking a feast to a companion. My Einkorn Blueberry Scones have a magnificent lemon coat on top.

Einkorn Blueberry Scones with Lemon Glaze

Natively constructed blueberry scones made with einkorn flour and normally improved with maple syrup. The fundamental pleasantness and flavor comes from the lemon coat, so don't skip it.

MAKE THIS RECIPE

On the off chance that you love everything pumpkin, you'll need these Einkorn Pumpkin Scones. Try not to skirt the maple walnut coat - it truly makes them a tomfoolery treat.

CHAPTER 6

EINKORN PUMPKIN
SCONES WITH MAPLE
GLAZE

Pumpkin scones made with einkorn flour and normally improved with honey or maple syrup.

MAKE THIS RECIPE

10. Einkorn Biscuits

Flaky bread rolls are a wonderful source of both blessing and pain, and you can build their nourishment with einkorn flour. Hand crafted Einkorn Biscuits carry out rapidly and make delightful layers.I additionally took that recipe and changed it somewhat to make individual chicken pot pies.

Hand crafted Einkorn Biscuits

Simple to make hand crafted rolls made antiquated einkorn flour. These bread rolls are totally cushioned and furthermore superbly flaky.

MAKE THIS RECIPE

- Einkorn Flour Q&A
- Is einkorn the best flour?

Einkorn is an assortment of wheat. It's known as the most established assortment of wheat, or the principal wheat, making it an old grain. Dissimilar to current wheat, which had gone through hybridization, einkorn still holds to its unique properties and dietary benefits. In our work to make present day wheat "better" and more effective from a creation outlook (through hybridization, mono-trimming, and so forth), supplements have been lost. Einkorn has a lot higher protein content (30% more than current wheat) and less starch (15% not exactly present day wheat), alongside a higher centralization of minerals and flavor. Einkorn is likewise more straightforward to process. Einkorn is among the best wheat flours. This study contrasting einkorn versus present day wheat is interesting.

Could you at any point utilize einkorn flour for baking?

Indeed! Einkorn is one of the most incredible wheat flours to use for baking. It has a light, somewhat nutty flavor with incredible dietary characteristics (30% higher protein content than present day wheat, 15% less starch, high grouping of minerals). You can partake in your number one prepared merchandise without compromising sustenance or flavor. Cakes, breads, biscuits, cupcakes, flapjacks, and scones are probably the best prepared products to make with einkorn flour. You can utilize generally useful einkorn flour 1:1 for universally handy ordinary flour in the majority of these recipes.

Does einkorn flour cause irritation?

This review, Integrated Evaluation of the Potential Health Benefits of Einkorn-Based Breads, is a captivating report on the medical advantages of einkorn versus present day wheat. "The four breads having the best qualities were chosen, and the result of their assimilation was utilized to assess their mitigating impact utilizing Caco-2 cells. Our outcomes affirm the higher carotenoid levels in einkorn than in current wheats, and the adequacy of sourdough aging in keeping up with these levels... " Einkorn shows guarantee in being calming (contrasted with current wheat) and when matched with sourdough rehearses (sourdough pre-digests grains during the maturation cycle, find out more), einkorn might be mitigating and is simpler to process. In the event that you as of now have a sourdough starter, make my #1 sourdough einkorn banana biscuits.

Could you at any point utilize einkorn flour instead of regular flour?

Indeed, you can utilize einkorn flour instead of regular baking flour. I suggest utilizing generally useful einkorn, which has a portion of the wheat eliminated (not all). As per Jovial Foods, "Universally handy (einkorn) is a high-extraction, lighter flour that has had 20% of the grain and microbe eliminated subsequent to processing and will remain new longer." If you need to utilize entire wheat einkorn instead of regular baking flour, decline the flour sum by 1/4 cup. Permit a hitter made with einkorn flour to rest for 10 minutes prior to baking, as einkorn flour is slower to ingest fluid.

Is einkorn flour equivalent to regular baking flour?

Einkorn flour isn't equivalent to regular baking flour produced using hard white wheat berries. Einkorn flour is produced using einkorn wheat berries, an old grain. There are two sorts of einkorn flour: entire wheat einkorn and generally useful einkorn. Entire wheat einkorn flour is 100 percent of the ground einkorn grain. Generally useful einkorn flour has 20% of the wheat from the grain eliminated.

Is universally handy einkorn flour entire grain?

My #1 flour to use for baking is universally handy einkorn flour as it delivers light and cushy heated merchandise. Generally useful einkorn flour isn't entire grain; 20% of the wheat is taken out. This really makes generally useful einkorn flour simpler to process, making it ideal for better baking. Entire wheat einkorn flour is an entire grain.

THE END